CLASSIC WISDOM COLLECTION

TODAY'S QUESTIONS. TIMELESS ANSWERS.

Looking for time-tested guidance for the dilemmas of the spiritual life? Find it in the company of the wise spiritual masters of our Catholic tradition.

Be Not Afraid: Wisdom from John Paul II

Christ in Our Midst: Wisdom from Caryll Houselander

Comfort in Hardship: Wisdom from Thérèse of Lisieux

Courage in Chaos: Wisdom from Francis de Sales

Inner Peace: Wisdom from Jean-Pierre de Caussade

Intimacy in Prayer: Wisdom from Bernard of Clairvaux

Life's Purpose: Wisdom from John Henry Newman

Path of Holiness: Wisdom from Catherine of Siena

Peace in Prayer: Wisdom from Teresa of Avila

Secret to Happiness: Wisdom from John XXIII

Secrets of the Spirit: Wisdom from Luis Martinez

A Simple Life: Wisdom from Jane Frances de Chantal

Solace in Suffering: Wisdom from Thomas à Kempis

Strength in Darkness: Wisdom from John of the Cross

Secret to Happiness

CLASSIC WISDOM COLLECTION

Secret to Happiness

Wisdom from John XXIII

Compiled and with a foreword by Donna Giaimo, FSP

BOOKS & MEDIA
Boston

Library of Congress Cataloging-in-Publication Data

John XXIII, Pope, 1881-1963.
  [Works. Selections. 2014]
  Secret to Happiness: Wisdom from John XXIII / compiled and with a
foreword by Donna Giaimo, FSP.
     pages cm. -- (Classic wisdom collection)
  Includes bibliographical references.
  ISBN-13: 978-0-8198-9025-2
  ISBN-10: 0-8198-9025-1
  1. Christian life--Catholic authors. I. Giaimo, Donna, editor of
compilation. II. Title.
  BX1378.2.J66 2014
  248.4'82--dc23

                              2013045625

Published by Pauline Books & Media, 50 Saint Pauls Avenue, Boston, MA 02130-3491

Printed in the U.S.A.

www.pauline.org

Pauline Books & Media is the publishing house of the Daughters of St. Paul, an international congregation of women religious serving the Church with the communications media.

1 2 3 4 5 6 7 8 9   18 17 16 15 14

Contents

Foreword

I don't remember the occasion or even the speaker, but a story served as my introduction to Saint John XXIII. It couldn't have come at a better time.

I had recently entered the convent and, as a newbie to religious life, was pretty earnest in my efforts to become holy. Equipped with an idealism characteristic of youth, I set out to make myself a saint—preferably in three years or less. Yet the harder I tried, the wider the chasm seemed between the goal and my reality. In the daily examination of conscience I had been taught to make, the meager number of "victories" in virtue compared to the painfully obvious failings left me disconcerted. And anxious. The saints—at least those whose lives I had read up until then—made it seem so easy. Perhaps I was doing something wrong or wasn't trying hard enough. Or just maybe, I began to worry, I wasn't cut out to be a sister in the first place.

At some point in the midst of all this tormented soul-searching, someone told me a story about Pope John XXIII. It seems that after his election, the new pope had trouble sleeping. One night John woke with a start, his thoughts flying to a particularly thorny issue. After wrestling with it a few minutes, he groggily thought to himself, *I'll have to take this up with the Pope in the morning.* Content with the thought, his eyelids drifted closed, only to snap open a moment later. *Wait a minute. I* am *the Pope! I guess I'd better take it up with God.*

There was something so human about this incident, and John's disarming ability to poke fun at himself, that I had to explore further. Sure enough, a quick scan of our library shelves led me to an out-of-print book our community had published, *Call Me John.* Released after the Pope's death, the book is certainly a moving tribute to a remarkable spiritual leader. But it was John's gentle humor and gift of holding himself lightly that spoke most eloquently to me.

Take, for example, his quick response to a visitor who asked how many people work at the Vatican. "About half," John quipped. Or the lighthearted way he put a nervous American photographer at ease: "Would you mind sending me a picture? No one ever sends me any pictures. . . ." Or his dry comment at the end of another trying papal photo session: "The good Lord has known for seventy-seven years that I would become pope. Could he not have made me just a bit more photogenic?"

As I read, I sensed there was something more at work here than easygoing charm. The stories demonstrated both confidence and humility, a certain comfortableness with himself and security in who he was. I wondered how he had gotten to this point. Had he been born with this stuff? A trip back to the library, this time for the book *Journal of a Soul*, provided the answer. John's own words showed me that through years of assiduous correspondence with grace, he had learned the secret to a happy life: losing oneself and finding God.

Born in 1881, Angelo Giuseppe—the future Saint John XXIII—was the third of thirteen children born to Marianna and Giovanni Roncalli. The Roncallis were poor farmers who lived in Sotto il Monte, near the Italian city of Bergamo. John avoided romanticizing those early years. As pope he once remarked that there were "three ways for a man to come to ruin: women, gambling, and farming. My family chose the most boring way."

The Roncalli children grew up in a faith-filled home. It came as no surprise when Angelo, nicknamed "the little priest" by his grade school friends, asked to enter the minor seminary at age eleven. He would spend the next twelve years in study and preparation for the priesthood, which took place on August 10, 1904.

A year after his ordination, Father Roncalli became secretary to the bishop of Bergamo and was assigned to teach at the diocesan seminary. When World War I broke out in 1914, he was briefly conscripted in the army, serving as a hospital orderly and military chaplain. His service ended in 1918, and he was appointed spiritual director of the seminary at Bergamo and, three years later, National Director of the Society for the Propagation of the Faith. Beginning in 1925 and continuing over the course of twenty-eight years, he served as apostolate delegate to Bulgaria, Turkey, Greece, and France. Pope Pius XII elevated him to the College of Cardinals and appointed him archbishop of Venice in 1953.

Five years later, Cardinal Roncalli attended the solemn consistory convened after the death of Pius XII. On October 28, 1958, Roncalli was elected pope, taking the name of John XXIII. At seventy-seven years of age, he was viewed by many as a transitional pontiff. He subsequently shocked the world when, only three months into his pontificate, he announced his desire to hold an ecumenical council for the purpose of renewing the Church so that it might offer a more credible witness to the Gospel in the modern world. Reaction to the news was not altogether favorable. "A council in 1963?" one Vatican official asked, appalled at the amount of work that would be required in such a time frame. "We can't possibly have a council in 1963."

"All right," Pope John responded smoothly. "We'll have it in 1962."

Time magazine would hail the Second Vatican Council as the single most important event of the twentieth century. John, who had conceived the idea as an inspiration from God (he sheepishly admitted that no one was more surprised by the proposal of a council than he), took no personal credit for it; he viewed himself simply as an instrument of the Divine will. As such, he was able to let go of his desire to see the work through to its completion. At the end of the Council's opening day, he wrote in his diary, "With the same calm I repeat: May your will be done with respect to my remaining in this primary position of service for whatever time and circumstances are left of my poor life—and I feel that death may approach at any moment—because the pledge to proceed, continue, and finish [the work] will be passed on to my successor."

Already suffering from the beginnings of stomach cancer when he wrote these words, "Good Pope John" died less than a year later, on June 3, 1963. John had offered his life for the good outcome of the Council, and the Lord was pleased to accept his offering.

—— ⌒ ——

In addition to the incomparable gift of the Second Vatican Council, John XXIII left us an extraordinary spiritual patrimony. From the age of fourteen until his death at eighty-two, he had kept a diary in which he recorded his journey in the spirit. Published after his death, *Journal of a Soul* ranks alongside other classic spiritual autobiographies. It offers insight into the intimate relationship John shared with the Lord and the process by which God gradually purified his heart. Invited into John's personal spiritual journey, we cannot help but draw inspiration for our own.

In his journal John lays bare his soul, recounting all—grace and insight, his desire to correspond and missteps along the way—with utter confidence in God's continuous action in his life. John was undoubtedly gifted by nature with an easygoing personality, yet his writings also show that interior peace was the result of a journey marked by spiritual discipline, the recognition of selfish tendencies, and an obedience that gave the Holy Spirit freedom to work in him. The outcome? He remained unswervingly optimistic and joyful throughout life, not only about his own reality but about the goodness he found in the world and in every person. "If God made the shadow," he is often quoted as saying, "it was to emphasize the light."

John was secure in God's love for him, and he allowed that love to define him. He had no trouble grasping who he was and who God was for him: "God is all, I am nothing." Such an admission prompted humility and trust. It helped him get up after repeated failures and give himself to God anew in a love forgetful of self. It also protected him his whole life from taking himself too seriously, a lesson I have tried to learn again and again since those first weeks spent trying to master convent life.

John had a distinctly playful way of sharing the lesson with others. He once visited the Hospital of the Holy Spirit in Rome, run by a community of sisters. The superior, undeniably excited by his visit, introduced herself: "Your Holiness, I am the Superior of the Holy Spirit."

"Congratulations, Sister," John beamed. "I'm just the Vicar of Jesus Christ."

Christians in every age can use John's advice (albeit paraphrased) to lighten up a bit. If we spend more time taking God and his promises—not ourselves—seriously; if we tear our gaze away from "us" and fix it on Christ, then like John we will find ourselves in happy dependence on God—a decidedly good place to be. We will hold everything, including ourselves, lightly because we will know we are grasped and held by God, and that this God who tenderly carries us will never let go. John shows us precisely how to experience the freedom, peace, and joy that come from this kind of knowledge.

I

What God Wants Me to Be

God, who sees me and enlightens me, keeps an eye on my slightest actions, even the almost imperceptible movements of my heart; on my immense poverty, the memory of sins committed, and of innumerable graces, past and present. All these things should keep me so habitually united to God, so delicate of conscience, that I have no need of other motives.

The precious and sublime conclusion of all the meditations of this first day [of retreat] is the great principle of indifference. In theory I work marvels in this regard, but in practice I am the one who makes least use of this principle. When something happens here that even indirectly touches me personally, my imagination and self-love torment me in an extraordinary way. Yet the keystone of the spiritual edifice is right here: to not do my own will but God's, to be habitually disposed to accept anything whatsoever, no matter how repugnant to my feelings and my pride.

In important affairs there is no difficulty; I will do nothing more or less than what the superiors and my spiritual father call for. The hard part is not doing things according to obedience, but conforming my intellect and my will to the counsel of my superiors, setting aside my particular views—even if apparently fair and holy—as well as inclinations of the imagination and of the other self.

No anxiety then, no castles in the air; few ideas, but just and serious, and fewer wishes. "One thing is necessary" (see Lk 10:42). Golden dreams of working in one way rather than another, fantastically colorful designs of what I can do tomorrow or next year or later—away with all of these!

I will be what the Lord wants me to be. It is hard for me to think of a hidden life, neglected, perhaps despised by all, known only to God; this is repugnant to my self-love. And yet, until I succeed in doing such violence to my pride that this obscurity becomes not only indifferent but welcome and attractive, I will never do all that God wants from me.

— Excerpt from *Il Giornale dell'Anima*,
spiritual exercises of December 9–18, 1903

My particular temperament, experience, and current circumstances lead me to adopt work that is quiet and peaceful, removed from the front lines, rather than activity that is aggressive, polemical, or combative. Well then, I do not want to become a saint by defacing an original painting in order to become an unsatisfactory copy of someone else with a character markedly different from mine. But this peaceful nature does not mean consenting to self-love, seeking my own satisfaction, or merely acquiescing in thoughts, principles, and attitudes. The usual smile upon my lips must conceal the inner struggle with selfishness, which is sometimes frightening, and, when necessary, embody the victory of the spirit over the weakening of the senses or of pride, so that God and my neighbor always have the best part of me. . . .

O my Lord, I am back today to offer you the precious chalice of my soul, sanctified by your anointing. Fill it with your virtue as you so appointed the apostles, martyrs, and confessors. Make use of me in something good, noble, and great—for you, for your Church, and for souls. I live, I want to live, only for this.

— Excerpt from Il Giornale dell'Anima, August 10, 1914

II

No Humility Apart from Jesus

When I think of the great mystery of Jesus's hidden and humble life during his first thirty years, I am always astounded and words fail me. Ah! It is quite evident that before such a shining example, judgments and ways of thinking—not only of the world but also of a vast majority of clergymen—disappear altogether or seem directly contradictory. As for me, I confess that I still cannot even form an idea of what humility is like. However much I study it, I seem to obtain only a semblance of humility; its real spirit, Jesus Christ's "love to be unknown," is known to me by name only. To think that our blessed Jesus spent thirty years of his life in obscurity, and he was

God. And he was the splendor of the substance of the Father. And he had come to save the world. And he did all this only to show us how necessary humility is and how it must be practiced. And I, such a great and exceedingly miserable sinner, think only of being pleased with myself and congratulating myself over good results, all for a little worldly honor. I cannot conceive even the holiest thought without interference from concerns about my own reputation with others. However much I adopt devotion and a spirit of charity and sacrifice, I can't yearn for the purest ideal without the other "I" stepping in, wanting to show off, to be admired by those near and far, by the whole world if it were possible. And worst of all, when it comes to true hiddenness, which Jesus Christ practiced and taught me, ultimately I do not know how to adapt myself to it without the greatest effort. . . .

I feel that my Jesus is drawing nearer and nearer to me. During these days he has allowed me to plunge into the depths and be submerged in the realization of my wretchedness and pride, to show me my urgent need of him. When I am about to sink, Jesus, smiling and walking to meet me on the water, comes to save me. Just as Peter, I feel like saying to him: "Go away from me, Lord, for I am a sinful man" (Lk 5:8), but I am prevented by the tenderness of his heart and the gentleness of his voice: "Do not be afraid" (Lk 5:10).

Oh, near you I am no longer afraid of anything. I rest on your bosom, like the lost sheep; I hear the beating of your heart. Jesus, I am yours again, forever yours. With you I am truly great; without you, a fragile reed. I am a column of strength when I lean on you. I must never forget my own nothingness, so that I never depend on myself. Even when I am bewildered and humiliated, I must always cling to your heart with the greatest trust, because my poverty is the throne of your mercy and love.

"Good Jesus, I am always with you; never go far from me."

— Excerpt from *Il Giornale dell'Anima*,
spiritual exercises of April 1–10, 1903

III

I Am Nothing; God Is All

Who am I? What is my name? What are my titles of nobility? Nothing, nothing! I am a servant and nothing more. Nothing belongs to me, not even my life. God is my master, the absolute master over life and death. No parents, no relatives, no lords in this world: My true and only master is God.

So I live to obey God's slightest commands. I cannot move a hand, a finger, or an eye; I cannot look forward or backward unless God wills it. Before him I stand upright and motionless, like a boy soldier standing in attention before his superior, ready for anything, perhaps even to throw himself into the flames. This must be my duty my whole life long, because I was born for this; I am a servant!

I must always regard myself in this state of a servant. Therefore I do not have one single moment free to wait on myself, to serve my pleasure, my vanity, etc. If I do, I am no better than a thief, because I am stealing time that is not my own; I am an unfaithful servant, a wicked servant unworthy of hire. Woe to me! Yet this is what I have done. What confusion and embarrassment I feel! So much pride, arrogance, and presumption, and I do not even know how to be a servant.

O Lord my God, I recognize your rights over me. Forgive my infidelity. Evil inclinations often distract me from attending to your divine service. Not anymore. I bind myself to your service, and I am here before you like Saint Francis Xavier. Look at me, O Lord. "I am your servant, O LORD: give me understanding that I may learn your commandments" (see Ps 119:125, 73).

— Excerpt from *Il Giornale dell'Anima*,
spiritual exercises of December 10–20, 1902

IV

Personal Holiness
in the Real World

As a result of experience I am convinced of one thing: the concept of holiness that I had formed and applied to myself was false. In every single action, and in the little failings I immediately perceived, I used to call to mind the image of some saint whom I intended to imitate down to the smallest detail, like an artist who makes an exact copy of a painting by Raphael. I always said: In this case Saint Aloysius would do such and such, or he would not do this or that, etc. It turned out, however, that I could never achieve what I had imagined I would be able to do, and this worried me. The method was wrong. I must take the substance of the saints' virtues, not the accidents. I am not Saint Aloysius, so I should not try to become holy the way he did, but rather according to my own way of being, my own character, my own circumstances. I do not have to be the pale, dried-up reproduction of even the most perfect model. God wants us to follow the examples of the saints, assimilate the vital substance of their virtues, convert it into our own blood, and adapt it to our own unique habits and special circumstances.

— Excerpt from *Il Giornale dell'Anima*, January 16, 1903

❧

Recent falsehoods have attempted to undermine the concept of holiness. They have distorted this concept; colored it in lively shades perhaps only tolerated in a novel, but which, practically speaking, are out of place in the real world. To know how to humble oneself constantly, destroying within and around oneself what others seek praise for from the world; to keep alive in one's own heart the flame of a most pure love for God, above and beyond weak, earthly affections; to give all, to sacrifice oneself for the good of others, with humility and love for God and one's neighbor; to follow faithfully the roads Providence indicates, which lead elect souls to fulfill their special mission. This is holiness.

— Excerpt from the essay *Il Cardinale Cesare Baronio della Congregazione dell'Oratorio, bibliotecario di Santa Romana Chiesa* (The life and works of Cardinal Caesar Baronius of the Congregation of the Oratory, librarian of the Holy Roman Church), written in 1908

❧

The ideal of holiness, smiling amid tribulations and the cross, is always with me. Interior calm founded on the words and promises of Christ produces an imperturbable serenity that is reflected in one's face, words, and character—the exercise of all-winning charity. We feel renewed energies, both physical and spiritual, sweetness to the soul and health to the body (see Prov 16:24). To live in peace with the Lord, to feel pardoned and in turn to pardon others.

— Excerpt from *Il Giornale dell'Anima*, November 28, 1940

V

Letting Go
of What Others Think

The thought of my examinations troubles me. I do not know how to present myself to my professors, to the whole teaching staff gathered together, to show what I have studied. But what will my soul do—poor, lonely sinner—before the whole heavenly court, before Jesus, the divine and strictest judge? At the very thought of this the saints trembled with fear, hiding in deserts—and they were saints. How silly of me then! I am afraid when there is nothing to be afraid of; and when there is something to be frightened about, I never even think of it. So, be a bit more objective. Less fear of exams down here and a greater diligence to acquire merits and perform good works, to make God's judgment less fearful.

One more observation: Why so much anxiety and trepidation over the outcome and success of my studies? Deep down, it all comes down to caring about what public opinion may say of me, because I am a slave to the judgment of men, a slave to my self-love. What foolishness! What does the judgment of men matter to me? Is it they who will reward me? Is God not the end of my efforts? . . .

Self-love! What a problem it is, when one stops to think about it! Who has ever defined what it is? What philosopher has ever occupied himself with it? It is the most important problem we struggle with, a fundamental problem, and who cares? Yet, as I am seeing in the meditations of these days, Jesus Christ in his great teachings is constantly showing us how we must fight this deadly enemy that corrupts all our actions. . . .

O sweet Jesus, I place myself at your feet, sure as I am that you will know how to achieve what I cannot even imagine. I want to serve you right where you want me, at any cost, with any sacrifice. There is nothing I know how to do; I do not know how to humble myself. This alone I know how to say, and I tell you so firmly: I want to be humble. . . .

— Excerpt from *Il Giornale dell'Anima*,
spiritual exercises of December 9–18, 1903

I confess that when it seems to me I really am following my heart's desire with simplicity and purity of intention, glad to give my post to whoever would want to fulfill it as well as or better than myself, even a hint of criticism from my brothers leaves me very bitter. I am wrong in being bitter and wonder why it disturbs me. Courage, my soul, this is only a bit of rain and snow. What will you say when a storm of criticism and opposition arrives? It is important to prepare myself for it. O Lord, *da mihi animas, cetera tolle* [give me souls; take away the rest]. I will also accept opinions, good or dubious, that others have or spread about me.

— Excerpt from his personal diary,
entry dated January 30, 1917

VI

All Success Comes from God

How many general and particular graces [I have received] in these ten years [of priestly ordination]! In the sacraments, received and administered, in the manifold and varied exercise of my ministry, in words and works, in public and in private, in prayer, in study, amid the small difficulties and crosses, successes and failures. . . . The Lord has indeed been faithful to the promise he made to me on the day of my ordination in Rome, in the Church of Santa Maria in Monte Santo, when he said to me: "No longer do I call you a servant . . . but a friend" (see Jn 15:15). Jesus has been a real friend to me, sharing with me all the sacred intimacies of his heart. When I think of all that he knows about me and sees in me, I would not be sincere if I did not admit to feeling a great satisfaction of spirit. In the field where I sowed and worked, there are a few ears of corn, enough perhaps to make a small bunch. May you be blessed, my Lord, because it is all due to your love.

For my own part, I can only feel embarrassed that I have not done more, that I have reaped so little, that I have been a wild and barren ground. With all the grace that I received, even with much less, others would already be holy! How many good desires have not yet borne fruit! My Lord, I acknowledge my deficiencies, my profound misery; may you be my pardon and mercy.

Beside the feeling of satisfaction and the need for forgiveness, the sentiment of gratitude sweeps through me. Everything, O Lord, has been accomplished for your glory; may you be thanked now and always.

But the overriding thought that occupies my spirit today, joyful at having been a priest for ten years, is this: I do not belong to myself or to others; I belong to my Lord, for life and for death.

— Excerpt from *Il Giornale dell'Anima*, August 10, 1914

O my Jesus, how I thank you for having kept me steadfast to this principle: "From me, as from a living fountain, the humble and the great, the poor and the rich, draw the water of life" [*Imitation of Christ*, III, IX, 6]. Ah, I am among the humble and the poor. In Bulgaria the difficulties of my circumstances, even more than those caused by men, and the monotony of a life interwoven with daily scratches and jabs cost me much in mortification and silence. But your grace sustained my inner joy, helping me to hide my apprehensions and discomforts. In Turkey the commitments springing from my pastoral concerns were a torment and a joy for me. Could I not, should I not, have done more—with more decided effort —and gone against the inclination of my nature? Did the search for calm and peace, which I considered more in accord with the Lord's spirit, not perhaps conceal a certain unwillingness to take up the sword and a preference for what was easiest and most convenient, even if gentleness is defined as the fullness of strength? O my Jesus, you scrutinize all hearts: the exact point at which the search itself for virtue can lead to fault or excess is known to you alone.

I feel it is right not to boast of anything but to attribute everything to your grace. . . . And my Magnificat is therefore complete, as it should be. I really like the expression "my merit, your mercy" and the words of Saint Augustine: "By crowning our merit, you crown your own gift."

Again, thank you endlessly, my Jesus.

— Excerpt from *Il Giornale dell'Anima*, April 6, 1950

I hardly know what to linger over more: how "I was glad when they said to me . . ." [Ps 122:1], with all that follows, or my sense of bewilderment, which inspires feelings of humility and abandonment in the Lord. It is he who has truly done everything, and done it without me, for I could never have imagined or aspired to much. I am also happy because this humility and poverty do not cost me great effort but come easily to my innate temperament. What should I be vain or proud about, my Lord? Is not "my merit" all "God's mercy"?

— Excerpt from *Il Giornale dell'Anima*, notes from 1953

VII

Being a Sinner

The advice of ancient philosophers—"Know your-self"—was already a good foundation for an honest and commendable life. It served for the regular exercise of humility, which is the primary virtue of great men. For the Christian, for the ecclesiastic, the thought of being a sinner does not at all mean depression of spirit, but confident and habitual abandonment in the Lord Jesus who has redeemed and pardoned us; it means a lively sense of respect for our neighbor and for souls, and safeguard against the danger of becoming proud of our successes. If one stays in the secret of one's intimate penitent cell, it will not only be a refuge for the soul who truly finds itself—along with peace of decision and action—but will also be a furnace igniting within oneself a livelier zeal for souls, pure intentions, and a mind free from preoccupations about success, which are external to our apostolate.

David needs the shock of the prophet's voice saying: "You are the man!" [2 Sam 12:7]. But afterward his sin is always present, always before him, as a continuous admonishment: "My sin is always before me."

Father Segneri wisely points out that it is not necessary to remember the exact delineation of every single sin, which would be neither profitable nor edifying, but it is well to bear in mind the memory of past weaknesses as a warning to holy fear and zeal for souls. How frequently the thought of sins and sinners recurs in the liturgy! This is even truer of the Eastern liturgy than of the Latin, but it is well expressed in both: "My sin is always before me," just as the sins of men and women were to Jesus in his agony at Gethsemane, as they were to Peter at the peak of his teaching, as to Paul in the glory of his apostolate, and as to Augustine in the splendor of his universal learning and episcopal sanctity.

Woe to those unhappy persons who, instead of keeping their sin before their eyes, hide it behind their backs! They will never free themselves from past or future evils.

— Excerpt from *Il Giornale dell'Anima*, November 26, 1940

VIII

Overcoming Self-love

Thus must our life be: to examine ourselves, to humble ourselves always, and to continue with new courage along the way the Lord has called us. This is how the lives and fruitful activities of the saints unfolded. We must be ready and willing to see our ego wounded. When we have allowed ourselves to be humbled, to be reduced to nothing in the hands of God, it is precisely then that the Lord uses us to confound the strong, to accomplish his wonderful works.

— Excerpt from a letter to G. Testa, December 29, 1907

The complete separation from oneself, the constant preoccupation to seek nothing but God in everything—his glory, his Church—is a great guarantee of success in our various ministries. I force myself to hold onto these principles, and I know, with great pleasure, that the Lord helps and blesses me.

— Excerpt from a letter to D. Spolverini, December 29, 1919

———— ❧ ————

At first [I felt] a sense of deep aversion for the new office, because it seemed unsuited to my tendencies and habits. Then [I felt] an interior struggle between the meaning, which seems sincere, of the *adveniat regnum tuum, fiat voluntas tua* [your kingdom come, your will be done] on the one hand, and self-love and reasons of the heart on the other. Lastly, [I felt] a flash of light holding me in balance and persuading me that it is for this particular ministry that the Lord is calling me.

— Excerpt from a letter to P. Giobbe, December 21, 1920

———— ❧ ————

Readiness to sacrifice, which the Lord wants from everyone and particularly in the measure he wishes, must be a great lesson and advice for me. This is sincere and sure devotion. Not only shedding tender tears during times of prayer, but having a perfect readiness of will for any divine service. "My heart is ready, O God, my heart is ready" [see Ps 57:7], for much or for little, to know what God wants and what God does not want, which therefore must not be done. How much delusion there is on this point! We easily shape for ourselves ways of serving the Lord that really are simply ways of expressing our own taste, our own ambition, our own whim. "Your proud heart has deceived you, you that live in the clefts of the rock" (Obad 3). In God's service you hardly know how to take one step outside your hole in which, like a tarantula, you take refuge from the ravages of time, and yet you like to persuade yourself that you could fly like an eagle if you were called to the mountains or to the seas. In your devotion you deceive yourself, and you are not even aware of it. Let the readiness of your will be seen in works done to fulfill the will of the Lord, as this is noted day by day, and do not demonstrate this readiness merely with fervent sighs.

— Excerpt from *Il Giornale dell'Anima*, November 30, 1940

IX

The Power of Goodness

"Do good—that is, be good—and you will always be surrounded by cheerful faces." These words shed light on our whole life.

To do good means giving worthy witness to Jesus, the Son of God and Son of Mary, the universal Teacher and Savior of the world.

No knowledge, wealth, or human power is more effective than a good nature, a heart that is gentle, friendly, and patient. The goodhearted person may suffer embarrassments and opposition, but he or she always wins in the end because this person's goodness is love, and love conquers all.

Throughout life, and especially at its end, the most joyous compliment is always the same: "He was so good; she had such a kind heart." And the person's name brings joy and blessing.

It is a mistake to think that kindness, that is, true friendliness, is simply a minor virtue. It is a great virtue because it denotes self-control and disinterested intention, along with keen love of justice. It is the expression and splendor of fraternal love, in the grace of Jesus. It is the way to attain human and divine perfection.

— Excerpt from *Scritti e Discorsi del Card. Angelo Roncalli, Patriarca di Venezia*, Vol. II: 1955–1956

——— ∾ ———

Nothing is more excellent than goodness. The human mind may look for other outstanding gifts, but none of these can be compared to goodness. It possesses the same nature as the Son of God himself, who became man, and it is the essence of all he taught us by word and deed: the exercise of fraternal love and patience, of constancy in compassion and fortitude, in the interior discipline of our own characters and in our social relationships, just as he told us.

Jesus did not say to us: Learn from me, for I am the Son of the heavenly Father. He did not show us how to create heaven and earth, or to clothe the sun in its mantle of splendor, but how to be meek and lowly of heart. This is the very foundation of goodness. When we understand the secret of goodness and have made it our own, we will have found the surest way of overcoming the difficulties and failures of our earthly life.

— Excerpt from *Discorsi, Messaggi, Colloqui del Santo Padre Giovanni XXIII*, Vol. II: 1959–1960

X

Adopting the Gentleness of Christ

"Take my yoke upon you, and learn from me; for I am gentle and humble in heart, and you will find rest for your souls. For my yoke is easy, and my burden is light" (Mt 11:29–30).

A Christian's entire strength is contained in these words. As you know, a yoke is borne by a pair of oxen. What an honor, what an unspeakable joy, to think of our shoulders bowed and harnessed with the shoulders of Christ under the very same yoke!

Remember: "Learn from me; for I am gentle and humble in heart"! Learn from Jesus, the Son of God, not how to create the world or launch the stars on their rapid, brilliant courses—not to rule and direct the destinies of nations—but to be gentle and humble in heart. Oh, what a mystery in the life of perfection, a mystery of grace and glory!

"Nothing is harsh for the gentle," wrote Saint Leo the Great, "nothing is hard for the humble." The secret of true greatness and of the miraculous success of men and saints is found in these words.

Let us pause here. Saint Augustine includes for us his own gentle counsel: "All who have learned from the Lord Jesus to be gentle and humble in heart make progress in perfection more by praying and meditating than by reading or listening" (Epist. 112).

> — Excerpt from *Scritti e Discorsi del Card. Angelo Roncalli,*
> *Patriarca di Venezia,* Vol. I: 1953–1954

❧

Strength of character is first and foremost a strength within ourselves, the strength we need when we are trying to understand our own nature, so that we may make use of its many resources and gifts in unstinting service of God and souls, and at the same time discover our own failings and make good what is lacking in ourselves by long and patient exercise of the virtues, fostered by trust and self-surrender in God.

It keeps us humble, for it puts us continually in mind of our own limitations and inadequacy. It is the mother of meekness and the gate of obedience, that sound school of learning for the strong of soul. By it we bend our stubborn nature that we may become more useful servants; we take ourselves completely in hand so as to acquire the gentleness of spirit that draws people to God; we defeat the power of our own nature so that the power of Christ may dwell in us (see 2 Cor 12:9).

— Excerpt from an address given to representatives of religious orders and congregations of women in Rome, January 29, 1960

XI

Leaving the Future to God

Preoccupations about the future stemming from self-love delay the work of God in us and hamper his purposes, even failing to promote our material interests. I need to be daily vigilant on this point, because I anticipate struggling with my pride years from now, and perhaps soon. Let whoever wishes to, pass and go on ahead of me; I stand here where Providence has placed me, without anxieties, leaving the way free for others.

— Excerpt from *Il Giornale dell'Anima*, August 10, 1914

This is what the Lord wants from us: only to begin. Then it is his task to carry it out with power and with calm, to multiply, to finish. The measure of God's effective involvement in our works corresponds to the spirit of simplicity and humility with which we begin them. We must therefore make up our minds and begin with pure intentions, a simple and humble heart, and the utmost trust in the Lord. He in turn will assist us, even in unexpected and miraculous ways.

— Excerpt from a letter to L. Bugada, December 11, 1927

"Whoever trusts in God will not be diminished" (see Sir 32:28). All that has happened in my poor life during these three months never ceases to amaze and confuse me. How many times I have had to renew my good resolution not to worry about my future or try to attain anything for myself!

Here I am now in Paris after Istanbul, having overcome—quite happily, it seems to me—the initial difficulties of insertion. Once again [my motto] *Oboedientia et Pax* [Obedience and Peace] has brought blessing. Here is everything I need in the form of interior mortification, in pursuit of a more profound humility and trusting abandonment, in order to consecrate to the Lord, for my own sanctification and for the edification of souls, the years I still have to live and serve holy Church.

— Excerpt from *Il Giornale dell'Anima*,
retreat during holy week, March 26–April 2, 1945

———— ❦ ————

I must not hide the truth from myself: I am decidedly on my way to old age. My mind reacts and almost rebels, for I still feel so young, eager, agile, and fresh. But just one look in the mirror stuns me. This is the season of maturity; I must produce more and better, reflecting that perhaps the time allotted me to live is brief, and that I am already near the doors of eternity. At this thought Hezekiah turned to the wall and wept. I do not weep.

No, I do not weep; I do not even want to go backward in time in order to do things better. I leave to the Lord's mercy whatever I have done, badly or less well, and I look to the future, brief or long as it might be here below, because I want it to be sanctified and sanctifying.

— Excerpt from *Il Giornale dell'Anima*,
retreat during holy week, March 26–April 2, 1945

———— ❦ ————

Last night I received a telegram from Vatican City telling me that the Holy Father has appointed me papal nuncio to France. I could not believe it since I never thought myself worthy of such a great honor and heavy responsibility. . . . I cannot tell you how I feel. There is a deep distrust and fear of myself and of my strength to bear such a heavy burden, and at the same time a great confidence in the Lord. He will surely help me, because I have never desired or even dreamed of this position. . . . As long as we are without pretense, God uses humble creatures to work out the design of his glory. Now I have a much greater need to grow in holiness, and your prayers will be a big help!

— Excerpt from a letter to his family, recorded in
Lettere ai familiari, p. 654

❧

. . . I am beginning my direct ministry at an age—seventy-two years—when others finish theirs. *I find myself on the threshold of eternity.* My Jesus, chief Shepherd and Bishop of our souls, the mystery of my life and death is in your hands, close to your heart. On the one hand I tremble at the approach of my last hour; on the other hand I trust in you and only look forward day by day. . . .

I do not desire, I do not think of anything else but to live and die for the souls that have been entrusted to me. . . . For the few years remaining of my life, *I want to be a holy shepherd* in the full meaning of the word. . . . But I will continue on my own road and with my own temperament. Humility, simplicity, adherence to the Gospel in word and works, with courage, meekness, impregnable patience, paternal and insatiable zeal for the good of souls. . . .

Sometimes the thought of the short time that remains to me would stem my zeal. But with the Lord's help I will not give in. I neither fear to die nor refuse to live. The Lord's will is still my peace.

— Excerpt from *Il Giornale dell'Anima*, notes from 1953

XII

Confidence in God's Love

In the midst of all work . . . I am very content. I have no idea why the Lord loves me so much. *Caritas Christi urget nos* [the love of Christ urges us on], as it did Saint Paul; when it fills the soul, little as it may be, it instills so much delight that one can desire nothing better on earth.

— Excerpt from his personal diary, entry dated March 19, 1917

The Lord's passion and resurrection indicate two lives for us: one that we barely live, the other for which we long.

Is Jesus, who deigned to put up with this poor earthly life for our sake, not able to give us the life we desire? He wants us to believe this, to believe in his love for us and in his eagerness to share with us his own riches, as he once chose to share our poverty. It was because we all have to die that he chose to die, too.

We know this already: our end and our beginning, birth and death. This is common knowledge, clear for all to see in our own sphere. Our sphere is this earth; the sphere of the angels is heaven. Our Lord came from one sphere to the other, from the realm of life to the realm of death, from the land of delight to the land of toil and sorrow.

He came to bring us his gifts and to bear our sufferings with patience; to bring us his gifts in secret and publicly to accept our wretched lot; to show himself as a man and to conceal his divinity; to appear in the flesh, while the Divine Word was obscured from our eyes. The Word was hidden but not silent: it taught us to endure in patience.

— Excerpt from *Scritti e Discorsi del Card. Angelo Roncalli, Patriarca di Venezia*, Vol. III: 1957–1958

~∾~

"It is that very Spirit bearing witness with our spirit that we are children of God" (Rom 8:16). Don't you consider it quite something to be the children of God? This confidence, often present in our hearts without our knowing how to account for it, is the inexhaustible source of our joy and the most solid foundation of true devotion, which consists in desiring everything that is full and loving service to the Lord. It is essential that this desire be prompt and effective. That it be a source of enjoyment—that is, of tender affection, sweetness, delight, and joyfulness—is also important, but accidental and secondary. The sense of the Lord's goodness to us, and of our poverty, makes us happy and sad at the same time. But the sadness is lessened too: it becomes a stimulus for our apostolate in the service of all that is ideal and noble, to make Jesus Christ known, loved, and served, and to take away the sins of the world.

— Excerpt from *Il Giornale dell'Anima*, November 28, 1940

I consider it a sign of the great mercy the Lord Jesus has for me that he continues to give me his peace and external signs of grace as well, which, I am told, explain the resilience of my calm, making me enjoy, in every hour of my day, a simplicity and gentleness of spirit that keep me ready to leave all and set off at a moment's notice for eternal life.

My defects and my miseries, "my countless sins, offenses, and negligences" for which I offer my daily Mass, are reasons for continued interior abasement that do not allow me to exalt myself in any way; but neither do they weaken my confidence, my abandonment in God, whose caressing hand I feel upon me, sustaining and encouraging me.

Nor do I ever feel tempted to vanity or complacency. "What little I know about myself is enough to confound me." . . .

"In you, O Lord, have I hoped; let me never be confounded."

At the start of my eightieth year this is what is important: to humble myself and lose myself in the Lord, and to stand in confident expectation of his mercy, in order to open the door to eternal life. Jesus, Joseph, Mary, may I breathe forth my soul in peace with you!

— Excerpt from *Il Giornale dell'Anima*,
spiritual exercises of November 27–December 3, 1960

XIII

Optimism That Builds Up

It is a great grace that I understand that people's souls are indeed good. If they abandon the Church, a large part of the guilt belongs to us priests. If we are all holy and apostolic, the Italy of the future will truly again be ours in Christ. But courtesy, patience, and humility are needed. *Beati mites, quoniam possidebunt terram* [Blessed are the meek, for they shall inherit the earth]. The world is more evil than we think, but it is also better than we think. Instead of wasting long hours in continual whining and complaints that benefit no one, we priests have to work and seize the good wherever we find it, hold it up to the uncontaminated light of principles, and multiply it. I maintain an incorrigibly optimistic outlook, and I do not know how to think otherwise. I never met a pessimist who accomplished any good.

— Excerpt from his personal diary, entry dated May 15, 1917

Since we are called to do good rather than to destroy evil, to build up rather than to tear down, I seem to find myself in the right place to continue always seeking the good without looking for different ways of understanding or judging life. Ah, the saints, the saints. . . . How they were practical, fervent, and good—above all good!

— Excerpt from his personal diary, entry dated July 10, 1917

Reasons for melancholy are never lacking—when were they ever absent in the history of the world?—because of the relentless fluctuation between sadness and joy in human life. Sometimes these combine and merge together, and when that happens we try in vain to separate them.

A wise person, a wise Christian, must do all one can to free oneself from sad thoughts, and at all times have recourse to those sources of comfort that transform suffering into motives of love, merit, and present and eternal joy.

The Mother of Jesus, who is our mother too—oh, how I love to connect these two titles!—is one of the richest sources of consolation for us, the richest after Jesus, who is by his very nature light and life. She is rich in comfort and joy and encouragement for all the children of Eve, who have become her children through Christ's redemptive sacrifice and will.

This explains the whole world's devotion to the Virgin, whom her saintly cousin Elizabeth truly hailed as "Blessed" in reply to Mary's confession of humility in the Magnificat, which remains the everlasting canticle of humanity redeemed, the song of the past, present, and future.

— Excerpt from *Scritti e Discorsi del Card. Angelo Roncalli, Patriarca di Venezia*, Vol. II: 1955–1956

The long experience of life teaches that it will avail us far more, for happiness of spirit, to discern the good in things and dwell upon that rather than to seek the bad and the flawed, emphasizing it thoughtlessly or, worse still, maliciously.

We know the teaching of Saint Peter in this regard. The Apostle Paul is even more emphatic. The most forceful words of all are those of Saint James, and he defies all comparison in his description of the wretchedness and damage done to truth and charity by too much [destructive] speech. The text of his Catholic Epistle on this matter [Jas 3:1–18] should be learned by heart and inscribed on the walls of all ecclesiastical dwellings.

— Excerpt from an address given to the clergy of Rome
during the first Roman diocesan synod, January 26, 1960

XIV

Simplicity, Sure Way to Sanctity

The surest way to my personal sanctification and successful service to the Holy See is the constant effort to reduce everything—principles, objectives, position, business—to the utmost simplicity and tranquility; to always prune my vineyard of useless leaves and tendrils and concentrate on truth, justice, and charity, but above all charity. Every other way of acting is pretension and a search for personal affirmation, which soon reveals itself as absurd and burdensome.

Oh, the simplicity of the Gospel, of the *Imitation of Christ*, of *The Little Flowers of Saint Francis*, of the most exquisite passages from Saint Gregory in the *Moralia: deridetur iusti simplicitas* [the simplicity of the just man is mocked] and what follows. How I enjoy these pages more and more, and how often I go back to them with interior pleasure! All the wise men of this world, all the wily ones of the earth, even Vatican diplomats . . . make such a bad impression when seen in the light of the simplicity and grace emanating from this great and fundamental teaching of Jesus and his saints! . . .

Lord Jesus, preserve in me the love and practice of this simplicity which, by keeping me humble, makes me more like you and draws and saves the souls of men.

My character is inclined toward compliance and to readily seeing the good side of people and things rather than criticizing and judging harshly. This, along with the considerable age difference—which gives me more experience and a deeper insight into the human heart—often cause me interior distress because of those around me. Any type of ill treatment or distrust shown toward anyone, but especially toward the humble, the poor, the lowly; every harsh and thoughtless judgment causes me pain and great suffering. I remain quiet, but my heart bleeds. My colleagues are good ecclesiastics. I appreciate their excellent qualities; I am very fond of them and they deserve every good. But I suffer much in relation to them. On some days and in some circumstances I am tempted to react strongly. But I prefer silence, believing it to be a more eloquent and effective instruction. Could this be a weakness of mine? I must, I want to keep bearing the weight of this light cross in peace, together with the already mortifying sense of my littleness. . . .

— Excerpt from *Il Giornale dell'Anima*,
notes from November 23–27, 1948

<hr>

"Let us give thanks" [see Is 38:15]. The ordinary extent of human life, seventy years, is now reached. I look over my seventy years, I must admit, "in bitterness of soul." Ah! I carry with me feelings of confusion and pain "for my countless sins, offenses, and negligences," for the little I have achieved and for all I could and should have done in service of the Lord, of holy Church, and of souls. But at the same time I cannot forget the wealth of grace and mercy that Jesus has lavished so generously upon me, in contrast to any merit of mine: Therefore "his praise shall continually be in my mouth" [Ps 34:2].

"Simplicity of heart and speech!" The older I grow, the better I note the dignity and triumphant beauty of simplicity in thought, manner, and speech. A tendency to refine and simplify what is complex: to render everything with the greatest spontaneity and clarity, without worrying about frills or artificial thought and speech.

"To be simple with prudence"—the motto is Saint John Chrysostom's. How much doctrine in two phrases!

Amiability, tranquility, and imperturbable patience! I must always remember that "a soft answer turns away wrath." What discouragement is created by a rough, snappish, or intolerant manner! Sometimes the fear of being underestimated as a person of little worth tempts one to put on airs and dominate somewhat. This is contrary to my nature. To be simple, without any pretense, requires nothing of me. It is a great grace that the Lord gives me: I want to preserve it and be worthy of it.

— Excerpt from *Il Giornale dell'Anima*,
Spiritual exercises of April 10–12, 1952

XV

Safe in God's Hands

In these days the good Lord has been pleased to help me understand better what it means to be a priest and how this understanding should orient my entire priestly life. I must always regard myself as being in the hands of God, as a victim ready to sacrifice myself—my ideas, my comforts, my honor, all that I have—for the glory of God, for my bishop, and for the good of my dear diocese: "as a living sacrifice, holy and acceptable to God" (Rom 12:1). I will accustom myself to reflect always on the lofty significance of these words. So, without resorting to extraordinary things, I will find a way to practice continual mortification, especially of my self-love and of my comforts, without complaining and without ever losing the joy in my soul, which will also shine externally through all my actions. I will especially think of this while I am celebrating Holy Mass and will unite myself to Jesus Christ, High Priest and divine victim for the whole world. How beautiful it would be to work untiringly, to suffer in silence the small daily disappointments, without ever losing my composure and always keeping fresh and alive the desire to suffer more and contribute better to the true good of the diocese, to please the good master Jesus Christ.

I have reread the brief notes that I still keep as a reminder of the Spiritual Exercises made in Rome when I was a cleric preparing for Holy Orders. O my Lord, do not let me forget the good resolutions of those days.

I remain always the same, a sinner insensible to the subtleties of your love; yet I still desire to work and to sanctify myself, so that I may soon do something useful for the Church.

The examples of your saints, whose lives I read, spur me on to courageously imitate them. O good Jesus, sustain me in my good resolutions and help me.

— Excerpt from *Il Giornale dell'Anima*, October 1908

I would like to speak from my heart to each one of you. . . .

The Son of God, in the sacrament of his love, has sanctified your senses with the touch of his own pure body. He has calmed the desires of your flesh, consoled you in your sorrows, soothed your angry heart, and strengthened your wavering resolutions. How long do you still have to live? You do not know. But whether your road is long or short, the Eucharist, like Elijah's loaf, will be your unfailing food; it will keep you good company on your way up the Lord's mountain.

There are some who have failed to respond to the Lord's command, perhaps for a long time now, and who for years have even ignored his Easter. What message do I have for them? Courage; take courage, my brother, my child.

The doors of the banquet hall are never closed. Every day is the right day for the lost sheep to return to the care of the tender shepherd, who invites and reaches out to it with great longing.

Any day, any week, a sinner may return to God.

— Excerpt from *Scritti e Discorsi del Card. Angelo Roncalli, Patriarca di Venezia*, Vol. III: 1957–1958

[The crucified Jesus] looks at me and I speak to him. In our long and frequent conversations during the night, the thought of the redemption of the world has appeared more urgent to me than ever: "I have other sheep that are not of this fold." These arms proclaim that he died for everyone—for everyone. No one is rejected from his love, from his forgiveness. . . . At this last hour I feel tranquil and I am certain that my Lord, in his mercy, will not reject me.

—Taken from remarks made shortly before
entering his final agony, May 31, 1963

XVI

Peace from Following God's Will

Your Bishop-Uncle cannot reveal many secrets to you, but he can tell you this: the effort, learned and cultivated since childhood, of seeking the Lord's will in absolutely everything and not my own will or pleasure, taking care with great simplicity not to rely on myself and trusting in the Lord for all things, has always kept me in peace and tranquility of spirit. And so, if I should hear of myself being appointed to the highest level in the governance or service of holy Church, without my having noticed it or imagined it, I would not be upset. If I do not succeed in something and it goes badly, I easily recognize my own misery; if I succeed and do so well, I owe it all to the Lord.

— Excerpt from a personal letter written to his niece in 1951

Peace is before all else an interior thing, belonging to the spirit, and its fundamental condition is a loving and filial dependence on the will of God. "You have made us for yourself, O Lord, and our hearts are restless until they rest in you" (Saint Augustine).

All that weakens, that breaks, that destroys this conformity and union of wills is opposed to peace. First of all and before all there is wrongdoing, sin. Peace is the happy legacy of those who keep the divine law. "Great peace have those who love your law" (Ps 118:165).

For its part, good will is the sincere determination to respect the eternal laws of God, to conform oneself to his commandments and follow his paths—in a word, to abide in the truth. This is the glory that God expects to receive from man.

— Excerpt from the Christmas message of December, 1959

XVII

Trust in God's Providence

The Lord . . . chooses the people and the circumstances, and he does not want us to interfere by what we do or think. Our greatness, our glory is found in our serene daily efforts—without excesses—marked by profound love for Jesus. In our daily effort to carry out the duty Providence has assigned us, we should give more attention to doing the little things well rather than trying to accomplish great works. Be especially careful to preserve humility, simplicity, and interior joy. In your work, the Lord reserves the fulfillment to himself, and he indicates the time and the circumstance, sometimes disposing that we remain in the dark. But he will fulfill.

— Excerpt from a letter to Sr. Cecilia, June 21, 1927

What little good I have been able to do in carrying out my apostolic mission is recorded in the book of life. God grant that in my last days it may be a cause of joy for me. As for my failings, faults, and limitations, if I have been negligent or have involuntarily offended anyone, please forgive me as good brothers do. I too am a man like you. But I can attest that although during these ten years my hands distributed much material assistance, sent by the Holy Father to satisfy public or private needs, to build churches to God, and to be used in other useful and worthy ways for the salvation of souls, none of these funds were used for my own convenience.

I depart a poor but contented man, for I have given everything away and leave all behind. The Lord will provide for my future needs. He will provide for me as he will provide for you too, my dear brothers. Boundless trust in divine Providence is our greatest consolation.

—From farewell remarks made upon leaving Bulgaria in 1935

We must trust the Lord. He makes us wait for him, but he always answers. Courage and joy always, therefore. *Caritas Dei et patientia Christi* [The love of God and the patience of Christ]. How I love these words! They mean more to me than the thought of living for a long or short time in this place or elsewhere.

— Excerpt from his personal diary,
entry dated November 25, 1931

XVIII

Humiliation Borne with Joy

My persistent pain, which is often a secret anxiety, is always the same old thing: not being able to keep up with all I have to do, and having to constantly try to overcome my natural sloth, which tends to make me tranquil and slow, although I am always moving. This suffering humiliates and almost saddens me. I must grasp and hold dear everything that may be a source of humiliation but without losing my interior peace and calmness. This is my torment. My not being able to get to things more quickly may be due to several reasons, for example, a real work overload, the particular circumstances of my position here and in Greece. But I must choose to attribute this state of things to my own insufficiency and "at least bear it patiently, if not joyfully," as Thomas à Kempis says (bk. III, chap. 57). Then there is that other sentence of his in the same book of *The Imitation*, that I must not consider myself truly humble until I recognize that I am truly inferior to everyone else.

The highest points of the spiritual life are firm, thanks be to God: absolute detachment from my own nothingness; to remind myself that, in the words of the Abrosian Mass, "I am the least of all, and a sinner"; to abandon myself completely to the Lord's will; to desire to live for nothing else but the apostolate and the service of holy Church. I must have no worries about my future; be ready for every sacrifice—even life itself, should the Lord consider me worthy—for divine glory and the accomplishment of my duty; have great spiritual fervor, in keeping with the mind of holy Church and the best tradition, without exaggeration of external forms or methods; pay attention to everything with mild and vigilant zeal, but always with much patience and gentleness, remembering what Cardinal Mercier quotes Gratry as saying that gentleness is the fullness of strength. And finally, I must always be familiar with the thought of death, which serves both to give eloquence and joy to life.

— Excerpt from *Il Giornale dell'Anima*,
spiritual exercises of October 25–31, 1942

The one who exalts us even before the world is God, and God alone. Every honor that comes to us should reflect God, or we must despise it. Does the Lord permit a small humiliation? So be it. Oh, if we only knew the great value of these humiliations! They have a very great influence on our entire spiritual life, and they leave very precious traces of good. Go before Jesus and tell him with sincere abandonment of spirit: O Jesus, I entrust myself to you. If you permit humiliations, I will be more than happy to find myself united to you, humiliated and scorned with you. When one is thrown to the ground in this manner, it is not possible to fall lower; one can only rise.

— Excerpt from a letter to G. Testa, June 18, 1912

XIX

Love of the Cross

B y divine grace I feel that I want to be truly indifferent to all that the Lord wishes of me regarding my future. . . . For some time now I have been reciting every morning after the Holy Mass—and I believe I say it with my heart—the prayer Saint Ignatius used to conclude his great meditation on the kingdom of Christ: *O aeterne Domine rerum omnium, ego facio meam oblationem* [O eternal Lord of all things, I offer myself as an oblation. . . . *Spiritual Exercises*, no. 98]. Truly, I find it difficult to say this prayer. But since I want to keep myself totally absorbed in the holy will of God and in the spirit of Jesus crucified and scorned, from now on I will make even the following profession daily: "O eternal Lord of all things, O heavenly Father, grant to me, your unworthy servant, that I may always be faithful to this desire: if it is a matter of equal praise and glory to your divine majesty, and to better imitate Christ our Lord so that I may grow more like him, I want to choose actual poverty with the poor Christ, and not riches; reproach with Christ who was reproached, and not honors; and I desire to be considered worthless and foolish for Christ who was once scorned, rather than being considered wise and prudent in this world" [*Spiritual Exercises*, no. 167].

The love of the Lord's cross attracts me all the more in these days. O blessed Jesus, do not let this be a spurt of flame to flicker out in the first shower of rain, but a burning, inextinguishable fire.

During this retreat I have found another beautiful prayer that corresponds very well with the circumstances of my situation, a prayer from Saint John Eudes. I humbly make it mine as well, and I hope that it is not too presumptuous of me. "O Jesus, my crucified love, I adore you in all your suffering. I ask your pardon for all the shortcomings I have committed until now in the afflictions you have been pleased to send me. I give myself to the spirit of your cross, and in this spirit, as in all love of heaven and earth, I embrace with all my heart, for your love, all the crosses of body and spirit that will come to me. And I promise to place all my glory, my treasure, and my happiness in your cross, that is, in humiliations, in privations and sufferings, saying with Saint Paul: 'May I never boast of anything except the cross of our Lord Jesus Christ' (Gal 6:14). As far as I am concerned, I do not want any other paradise in this world, except for the cross of my Lord Jesus Christ."

It seems to me that everything is leading me to habitually make this solemn profession of love for the holy cross. . . . The Lord wants me all for himself, along the "royal road of the holy cross." And it is along this path and no other that I wish to follow him. I like to repeat the image that Saint Francis de Sales used: *I am like a bird that sings in the thorny wood*; this must be a continual invitation for me. . . . The motto of my dear spiritual director during the first ten years of my priesthood returns to me: *Semper in cruce, oboedientia duce!* [Always in the cross, under obedience].

— Excerpt from *Il Giornale dell'Anima*,
Spiritual exercises of April 28–May 4, 1930

XX

Detachment and God's Will

It will even happen to you, that which seems to me to be the sign of God's direct action in our life. That is, to seem to be called to one form of service and instead, after achieving the first steps, receive another assignment. It turns all our energies elsewhere, in order to succeed in new and unexpected tasks, and to succeed better than we ourselves would have expected.

— Excerpt from a letter to G. Moioli, 1920

Find sweetness in doing everything in the will of the Lord. I almost no longer know where I left my own will. Now it is something like an amputated leg. It is no longer there, thanks be to God, but occasionally it makes itself felt due to changing temperatures or unpleasant weather.

—From an excerpt of a letter to N. Fressati, April 2, 1933

I received your confidential letter on the tenth of this month. I took enough time to confide in the Lord and reflect on it, but I did not need much time. In what Your Excellency proposes to me there is really nothing of my own will. So I repeat my episcopal motto, the one of Caesar Baronius, the well-loved disciple of Saint Philip Neri who every day would kiss the foot of Saint Peter and say: *"Oboedientia et pax."* The Holy Father may use me with perfect freedom of spirit. May Your Excellency be pleased to assure His Holiness that I have little regard for myself; for me everything is more than I deserve. Having renounced my personal preferences for so long makes everything easier and more serene for me, and it assures me of great peace. With all my heart I wish that the Lord might heal the Patriarch of Venice and give him a long life. But if I happen to succeed him, may the Lord make me worthy of meriting the ancient praise of Saint Mark, disciple and interpreter of Peter.

— Excerpt from a letter to the Substitute Secretary of State as recorded in *Giovanni e Paolo: due papi. Saggio di corrispondenza: 1925–1962*

XXI

Poverty in Spirit and in Fact

A few months ago I got a house and suitably furnished it. Nevertheless, perhaps now more than ever before, the Lord makes me feel the beauty and sweetness of the spirit of poverty. I am willing to give up everything on the spot, and without regrets. I shall endeavor, as long as I live, to keep this feeling of detachment from all that is mine, even from what I hold dearest.

I especially oblige myself to seek perfect poverty of spirit in absolute detachment from myself, never worrying about positions, career, distinctions, or anything else. Am I not already more than honored in the integrity of my priesthood and in a ministry not sought but entrusted to me by Providence and by the voice of my superiors? . . .

Oh, how true it is that for one who completely trusts the Lord, everything is provided! "Having nothing yet possessing all things" (see 2 Cor 6:10) is daily renewed before my eyes. I do not want debts, and I have none. I am always at a loss to provide for the future, but I always receive what I need, and sometimes more.

This ascertainment of divine assistance comforts me in my poverty, but it also constitutes for me another commitment to honor and hold true to my vocation, to cooperate "until the end" in the great work that Jesus has entrusted to me.

— Excerpt from *Il Giornale dell'Anima*,
Spiritual exercises of April 28–May 3, 1919

I already have two painful issues here amid all the splendor of ecclesiastical rank and the regard shown me as Cardinal and Patriarch: the meagerness of my revenue and the swarm of the poor with their requests for employment and financial help.

As for revenue, nothing prevents me from improving it, both for my own sake and that of my successors. But I love to bless the Lord for this poverty, which is a bit humiliating and often embarrassing. It makes me better resemble the poor Jesus and Saint Francis. And I am quite sure I will not die of hunger. O blessed poverty, which assures me of a greater blessing in everything else and in what is most important for my pastoral ministry!

— Excerpt from *Il Giornale dell'Anima*,
Spiritual exercises of May 15–21, 1953

XXII

Living in Abandonment

Today, January 18, the Feast of the Chair of Saint Peter, marks three years since I began under obedience the work as president for Italy of the Propagation of the Faith in the world. You have always been present to me, O my Lord Jesus, good and merciful: "Your decrees are very sure" [Ps 93:5]. With sorrow I left behind in Bergamo what I loved so much: the seminary, where the bishop had appointed my most unworthy self as spiritual father, and the house for the students, beloved of my heart. I threw myself, heart and soul, into my new ministry. Here I must and will remain, without thinking, without looking, without aspiring to something else, especially since the Lord gives me indescribable delights here.

Anyone who judges me from appearances considers me a calm and steady worker. Yes, I work—always; but deep in my nature there is a tendency toward laziness and distraction. I will fight this tendency vigorously, with the help of God. . . . I will take special care not to procrastinate but do at once what needs to be done promptly. In everything, however, I must keep and impart to others that calmness and composure with which alone things can be done and done well. I will not worry if others are in a hurry. Whoever is always running, even in ecclesiastical matters, never gets very far.

— Excerpt from *Il Giornale dell'Anima*,
spiritual exercises of January 13–19, 1924

I too have had my plans and my visions; I have found and I still find them natural. If I were to go back to relive the past ten years of my life, I believe I would do the same. However, I have abandoned myself into the arms of obedience. For the most part my dreams and visions have disappeared. God has disposed of me differently.

— Excerpt from a letter to G. Testa, August 5, 1910

On the first day [of retreat] I stayed with the theme of holy detachment. On the second day I made my confession to my usual excellent confessor, Father Alberto. I remained content and very tranquil and quiet of heart. Once more I reviewed the best resolutions of my episcopal life, and I renewed them with all the fervor the Lord was pleased to give me. I consider myself wretched and miserable, but I persist in my resolve to sanctify myself at all costs, with calm and patience, with absolute abandonment in Jesus, the "shepherd and guardian of my soul" [see 1 Pet 2:25].

The general basis for my resolutions these days is expressed in the simple words of the *Imitation of Christ*: "Desire to be unknown and little esteemed." And with all of this no discouragement; indeed always be happy, always serene, always brave to the last hour. . . .

My prolonged time as papal representative in this country [of France] often causes me acute and intimate sufferings that I try to hide. But I bear all and will do so willingly, indeed joyfully, for the love of Jesus, in order to resemble him as closely as possible, to fulfill his holy will in everything, and for the triumph of his grace in the midst of these simple and good—but alas, so very unfortunate—people! All in the service of Holy Church and the Holy Father and for my own sanctification. "Lord, you know everything; you know that I love you" [Jn 21:17].

— Excerpt from *Il Giornale dell'Anima*, spiritual exercises of September 4–8, 1933

XXIII

The Primacy of Charity

L ove is all; love is at the foundation of civilization; love is the basis of all that Christ came to declare to the world. . . . Without love you may obtain temporary successes, or victories won by force, but afterward, and very soon, all will fall to the ground. This has been proved by our experience in recent years.

Let us love the Lord. Let us love one another.

We must know how to suppress the self and how to emphasize the unity, the social nature, of man. Saint Thomas says that man is a *social animal*, and this is true. Our own welfare is our brothers' welfare; it is that of others, of all men.

Be careful of misunderstandings: they crop up, challenge each other, and exchange blows. We must be on our guard against them. If they cannot be avoided, at least let us not nurture them or allow our imagination to exaggerate them. Let us try, forthrightly, to be the first to explain them away, to put things right once more, to untangle them and keep ourselves free from any resentful feelings.

Even among cultured and spiritual people there may exist a variety of opinions and viewpoints in matters open to discussion. This does not impair charity and peace, as long as we strive for moderation in manner and harmony of mind. Moreover, I will add that the Lord makes use of these misunderstandings to bring good about in other ways. As a result Paul and Barnabas separated because of young John Mark . . . and yet they were both equally righteous and holy. With souls like these everything is set right by the Lord's grace. But this does not alter the fact that we must watch out for misunderstandings and try to clear them away.

We can never forget those words of our Lord that astonished the world, when he said that it gives the heart more joy and peace to believe and renounce than to demand and receive.

— Excerpt from *Scritti e Discorsi del Card. Angelo Roncalli, Patriarca di Venezia*, Vol. IV: 1953–1958

Serenta conscientia puram offerre orationem—it is an exquisite word-picture of prayer, this phrase of à Kempis: "To offer, with quiet conscience, pure prayer." So prayer is born of a quiet conscience, that is, a conscience that is neither elated by success nor cast down by tribulation of body or of spirit; that makes good use of every moment of time, directed in everything by obedience. It is manifested by sincerity of life and love of all humanity, by purest charity, charity modeled on Saint Paul's hymn of praise in his First Letter to the Corinthians. Charity, Saint Paul tells us, is patient, beneficent. It is not envious or insolent; not full of self-importance or ambitions; it is not given to self-seeking, impulses of anger, or evil thoughts; it takes no pleasure in injustice but is glad at heart in the possession of the truth; it will always tactfully cover things up; it sets no limit to its belief and hope; it will put up with anything (see 1 Cor 13:4–7).

From such a quiet, peaceful conscience flows a prayer that is pure, a prayer that is listening to God, speaking to God, silence in God, asking him for those things that are pleasing to him. Prayer of adoration and thanksgiving, more than prayer of petition. The Lord is well aware of our many needs!

— Excerpt from an address given to representatives of religious orders and congregations of women in Rome, January 29, 1960

XXIV

Comfort in Humility

Retreating into myself and reflecting on the various events in my humble life, I recognize that the Lord exempted me from the tribulations that make service to truth, justice, and charity so difficult and demanding for many people. I lived through my infancy and youth without noticing the poverty, without worrying about family, studies, or dangerous circumstances such as those I faced, for example, during my military service at the age of twenty, and during the Great War. . . .

Little and humble as I acknowledge myself to be, I was always warmly welcomed wherever I went, from the seminary in Bergamo and later in Rome, through the ten years of my priestly life near my bishop in my native city; from 1921 until now, 1961, that is from Rome and back to Rome, as far as the Vatican. O good God, how do I thank you for the gracious manner in which I was received wherever I went in your name, always in pure obedience, not to do my own but your will? "What shall I return to the LORD for all his bounty to me?" I know well that my answer, to myself and to the Lord, is always: "I will lift up the cup of salvation and call on the name of the LORD" [see Ps 116:12 and 13].

As I have already mentioned in these pages: if and when the "great tribulation befalls me," I must welcome it willingly; and if it delays its coming a little longer, I will continue to nourish myself with the blood of Jesus, with the addition of all those small or great tribulations that the good Lord may send me. Psalm 131 has always made, and still makes, a great impression on me: "O LORD, my heart is not lifted up, my eyes are not raised too high; I do not occupy myself with things too great and too marvelous for me. But I have calmed and quieted my soul, like a weaned child with its mother; my soul is like the weaned child that is with me" [Ps. 131:1–2]. Oh, how I love these words! But even if they were to agitate me toward the end of my life, my Lord Jesus, you will comfort me in my affliction. Your blood, your blood that I will continue to drink from your chalice, that is, from your heart, will be for me a pledge of eternal health and happiness. "For this slight momentary affliction is preparing for us an eternal weight of glory beyond all measure" (2 Cor 4:17).

— Excerpt from *Il Giornale dell'Anima*, written during a retreat at the end of his eightieth year, August 10–15, 1961

XXV

You Know That I Love You!

At the point of presenting myself before the Lord, One and Three, who created me, redeemed me, chose me to be his priest and bishop, and filled me with endless grace, I entrust my poor soul to his mercy. I humbly ask his pardon of my sins and deficiencies. I offer him what little good, even if paltry and imperfect, I was able to do with his help, for his glory, in service of holy Church, and for the edification of my brothers and sisters. And finally I implore him to welcome me, like a good and generous father, among his saints in eternal bliss.

The sense of my insufficiency and nothingness has always kept me good company, making me humble and tranquil, and giving me the joy of putting my best efforts into a continuous exercise of obedience and love for souls and for the interests of the kingdom of Jesus, my Lord and my all. To him be all the glory; for me and to my merit, his mercy. "God's compassion is my merit. Lord, you know all things: you know that I love you!" This alone is enough for me. . . .

The goodness shown my humble person by the many people I met on my journey has made my life serene. I remember well, in the face of death, each and everyone: those who have preceded me in the last step, those who will survive me, and those who will follow me. May they pray for me. I will do the same for them from purgatory or paradise, where I hope to be accepted not, I repeat, through my own merits but through the mercy of my Lord. . . .

In the hour of farewell, or better, until we meet again, I recall for everyone what counts most in life: blessed Jesus Christ, his holy Church, his Gospel—and in the Gospel particularly the *Our Father*, according to the mind and heart of Jesus—the truth and goodness of the Gospel, a goodness that is meek and kind, hardworking and patient, invincible and victorious.

My children, my brothers, *arrivederci*. In the name of the Father, of the Son, and of the Holy Spirit. In the name of Jesus our love; of Mary, our and his sweetest Mother; of

Saint Joseph, my first and favorite protector. In the name of Saint Peter, of Saint John the Baptist, and of Saint Mark; of Saint Lawrence Giustiniani and of Saint Pius X. Amen.

— Excerpt from *Il Giornale dell'Anima*, from his spiritual testament drafted during his years as patriarch of Venice and dated June 29, 1954

XXVI

The Decalogue
of Pope John XXIII [1]

1) Only for today I will seek to live the entire day positively, without wishing to solve the problems of my life all at once.

2) Only for today I will take the greatest care of my appearance: I will dress modestly; I will not raise my voice; I will be courteous in my behavior; I will not

---

1. The following is a compilation of spiritual maxims drawn from St. John XXIII's life and writings and presented in a homily by Cardinal Tarcisio Bertone on October 11, 2006.

criticize anyone; I will not claim to improve or to discipline anyone except myself.

3) Only for today I will be happy in the certainty that I was created to be happy, not only in the next world but also in this one.

4) Only for today I will adapt to circumstances without requiring all circumstances to be adapted to my own wishes.

5) Only for today I will devote ten minutes of my time to some good reading, remembering that just as food is necessary to the life of the body, so good reading is necessary to the life of the soul.

6) Only for today I will do one good deed and not tell anyone about it.

7) Only for today I will do at least one thing I do not like doing; and if my feelings are hurt, I will make sure that no one notices.

8) Only for today I will make a plan for myself: I may not follow it to the letter, but I will make it. And I will be on guard against two evils: hastiness and indecision.

9) Only for today I will firmly believe, despite appearances, that the good Providence of God cares for me as no one else who exists in this world.

10) Only for today I will have no fears. In particular, I will not be afraid to enjoy what is beautiful and to believe in goodness. Indeed, for twelve hours I can certainly do what might cause me consternation were I to believe I had to do it all my life.

Bibliography

Benigni, Mario and Zanchi, Goffredo. *John XXIII: The Official Biography*. Boston: Pauline Books & Media, 2001.

Cushing, Richard Cardinal. *Call Me John*. Boston: Daughters of St. Paul, 1963.

Donnelly, John P. (ed.). *Prayers and Devotions from Pope John XXIII*. New York: Image Books, 1969.

Feldman, Christian. *Pope John XXIII: A Spiritual Biography*. New York: The Crossroad Publishing Company, 2000.

Fesquet, Henri. *Wit and Wisdom of Good Pope John*. New York: P.J. Kennedy & Sons, 1964.

John XXIII, Pope. *Il Giornale dell'Anima*. Milan, Italy: Edizioni Paoline, 1965.

———. *Scritti e discorsi*. Milan, Italy: Edizioni Paoline, 1959.

Martin, James. *My Life with the Saints*. Chicago: Loyola Press, 2006.

Michaels, Louis. *The Stories of Pope John XXIII*. Springfield, Illinois: Templegate Publishers, 1964.

BOOKS & MEDIA

A mission of the Daughters of St. Paul

As apostles of Jesus Christ, evangelizing today's world:

We are CALLED to holiness
by God's living Word and Eucharist.

We COMMUNICATE the Gospel message
through our lives and through all
available forms of media.

We SERVE the Church
by responding to the hopes and needs
of all people with the Word of God,
in the spirit of St. Paul.

For more information visit our Web site:
www.pauline.org.

BOOKS & MEDIA

The Daughters of St. Paul operate book and media centers at the following addresses. Visit, call, or write the one nearest you today, or find us at www.pauline.org.

CALIFORNIA

3908 Sepulveda Blvd, Culver City, CA 90230	310-397-8676
935 Brewster Avenue, Redwood City, CA 94063	650-369-4230
5945 Balboa Avenue, San Diego, CA 92111	858-565-9181

FLORIDA

145 S.W. 107th Avenue, Miami, FL 33174	305-559-6715

HAWAII

1143 Bishop Street, Honolulu, HI 96813	808-521-2731
Neighbor Islands call:	866-521-2731

ILLINOIS

172 North Michigan Avenue, Chicago, IL 60601	312-346-4228

LOUISIANA

4403 Veterans Memorial Blvd, Metairie, LA 70006	504-887-7631

MASSACHUSETTS

885 Providence Hwy, Dedham, MA 02026	781-326-5385

MISSOURI

9804 Watson Road, St. Louis, MO 63126	314-965-3512

NEW YORK

64 W. 38th Street, New York, NY 10018	212-754-1110

PENNSYLVANIA

Philadelphia—relocating	215-676-9494

SOUTH CAROLINA

243 King Street, Charleston, SC 29401	843-577-0175

VIRGINIA

1025 King Street, Alexandria, VA 22314	703-549-3806

CANADA

3022 Dufferin Street, Toronto, ON M6B 3T5	416-781-9131

¡También somos su fuente para libros,
videos y música en español!